Patriotic

Recipes

About the Author

Laura Sommers is **The Recipe Lady!**

She is the #1 Best Selling Author of over 80 recipe books.

She is a loving wife and mother who lives on a small farm in Baltimore County, Maryland and has a passion for all things domestic especially when it comes to saving money. She has a profitable eBay business and is a couponing addict. Follow her tips and tricks to learn how to make delicious meals on a budget, save money or to learn the latest life hack!

Visit her Amazon Author Page to see her latest books:

amazon.com/author/laurasommers

Visit the Recipe Lady's blog for even more great recipes and to learn which books are **FREE** for download each week:

http://the-recipe-lady.blogspot.com/

Subscribe to The Recipe Lady blog through Amazon and have recipes and updates sent directly to your Kindle:

The Recipe Lady Blog through Amazon

Laura Sommers is also an Extreme Couponer and Penny Hauler! If you would like to find out how to get things for **FREE** with coupons or how to get things for only a **PENNY**, then visit her couponing blog **Penny Items and Freebies**

http://penny-items-and-freebies.blogspot.com/

Introduction

The summer is here! And with it comes the many patriotic holidays. Picnics, barbecues, camps and pool parties with fireworks and food! Memorial Day, Fourth of July Independence Day and Labor Day are all holidays celebrated during those lazy dog days. And what better way to celebrate then to make patriotic red, white and blue foods or foods that represent the spirit of patriotism.

So if you are planning a great patriotic party or are just looking for some fun celebration foods to make during a picnic or beach party then try some of these many patriotic recipes and enjoy!

Patriotic French Toast

Ingredients:

1 (10 oz.) package frozen strawberries, thawed
1 cup fresh blueberries
1 (8 oz.) package cream cheese, softened
2 cups confectioners' sugar
2 cups milk
2 eggs, beaten
1 tsp. vanilla extract
1/2 tsp. ground cinnamon
2 tbsps. butter

Directions:

1. Preheat an oven to 250 degrees F (120 degrees C).
2. Combine the thawed strawberries with their juice and the blueberries in a bowl; set aside. Beat together the softened cream cheese and confectioner's sugar until smooth; set aside. Whisk the milk, eggs, vanilla, and cinnamon in a shallow bowl.
3. Melt butter over medium heat in a large skillet or griddle.
4. Dip bread into egg mixture, coating thoroughly.
5. Cook until well-browned on both sides, about 5 minutes.
6. Place cooked slices on baking sheet and place in oven to keep warm until ready to serve.
7. Spread the cream cheese mixture over each slice of french toast, then top with 2 tbsps. of the fruit. Serve immediately.

Fourth of July Layered Gelatin

Ingredients:

1 (6 oz.) package cherry flavored gelatin mix
2 (.25 oz.) envelopes unflavored gelatin
2 cups boiling water
4 (.25 oz.) envelopes unflavored gelatin
1 cup boiling water
1 (14 oz.) can sweetened condensed milk
1 (6 oz.) package blue raspberry flavored gelatin mix
2 (.25 oz.) envelopes unflavored gelatin
2 cups boiling water

Directions:

1. Place cherry gelatin mix into a heatproof bowl, stir in 1 packet of unflavored gelatin, and mix with 2 cups of boiling water, stirring until the gelatin has dissolved and the mixture is clear, about 2 minutes.
2. Pour into the bottom of a 9x13 rectangular glass baking dish.
3. Place in refrigerator until completely cold and set, about 1 hour.
4. Sprinkle 4 packets of unflavored gelatin onto 1 cup of boiling water in a heatproof bowl, allow to stand for about 3 minutes, and stir until dissolved; mix in the sweetened condensed milk.
5. Allow to cool but not thicken, about 10 minutes; gently pour into a layer on top of the cherry layer.
6. Return to refrigerator and allow to chill completely, about 1 more hour.
7. Place blue raspberry gelatin mix and 1 packet of unflavored gelatin into a heatproof bowl, and mix with 2 cups of boiling water, stirring until the blue gelatin is clear, about 2 minutes.
8. Allow to stand and cool but not thicken, about 10 minutes; gently pour onto the white layer.
9. Chill in refrigerator until the dessert is firm and cold, about 1 hour.
10. Cut into squares to serve.

Patriotic Snowball

1 cup finely crushed ice (to slush consistency)
1/4 fluid oz. blue curacao liqueur
2 fluid oz. lemon-flavored vodka, divided
1/4 fluid oz. raspberry flavored liqueur

Directions:

1. Place half the ice into a bowl; divide the other half of the ice between 2 bowls (1/4 cup of ice in each).
2. Place blue curacao liqueur and 1/2 fluid oz. of lemon vodka into a bowl containing 1/4 cup of ice.
3. Mix well. Place raspberry liqueur and 1/2 fluid oz. of lemon vodka into the other 1/4 cup of ice and mix well. Mix the remaining 1 fluid oz. of lemon vodka into the bowl containing 1/2 cup of ice.
4. Layer the blue curacao-flavored ice into the bottom of a glass.
5. Place the lemon vodka-flavored ice over the blue layer; top with the raspberry-flavored ice.

Independence Cake Surprise

Extra-moist cake with buttercream icing with red, white and blue surprise inside layers.

Ingredients:

cooking spray
1 (18.25 oz.) package white cake mix
1 (3.5 oz.) package instant French vanilla pudding mix
3/4 cup water
3/4 cup vegetable oil
4 eggs
1 drop red food coloring, or as needed
1 drop blue food coloring, or as needed
1 cup butter-flavored shortening
1 cup unsalted butter at room temperature
1 tsp. salt
1 tbsp. clear imitation vanilla extract
8 cups confectioners' sugar
1 cup heavy cream

Directions:

1. Preheat oven to 350 degrees F (175 degrees C).
2. Spray 3 9-inch cake pans with cooking spray.
3. In a large bowl, beat the cake mix, instant pudding mix, water, vegetable oil, and eggs together with an electric mixer to form a smooth batter. Divide the batter equally into 3 smaller bowls; tint one bowl to your desired shade of red, and one to your desired shade of blue.
4. Pour each bowl into a prepared cake pan.
5. Bake in the preheated oven until the cakes are set and a toothpick inserted in the center of the cake comes out clean, 10 to 15 minutes.
6. The cakes will start to pull away from the sides of the pans when done.
7. Remove the cakes, allow to cool for about 10 minutes in the pans, and then turn out onto 3 separate pieces of plastic wrap set onto a work surface to finish cooling.
8. While the cakes are cooling, beat the butter-flavored shortening, butter, salt, and imitation vanilla extract in a large bowl with an electric mixer until creamy.
9. Mix in 1 cup of confectioners' sugar at a time, beating in each cup well before adding the next. Mix in the cream, 1 or 2 tbsps. at a time, until the frosting is smooth and spreadable.

10. To decorate, lift the red layer using the plastic wrap, and gently turn over and place onto a cake plate. Remove plastic wrap.
11. Generously frost the top of the red cake, then place the blue cake on top.
12. Frost the blue layer, then top with the white cake; use remaining frosting to frost the top and sides of the cake.

Red, White, and Blueberry Fruit Salad

Ingredients:

1 pint strawberries, hulled and quartered
1 pint blueberries
1/2 cup white sugar
2 tbsps. lemon juice
4 bananas

Directions:

1. Mix the strawberries and blueberries together in a bowl, sprinkle with sugar and lemon juice, and toss lightly.
2. Refrigerate until cold, at least 30 minutes.
3. About 30 minutes before serving, cut the bananas into 3/4-inch thick slices, and toss with the berries.

Patriotic Fruit Pizza

Ingredients:

2 3/4 cups all-purpose flour
1 tsp. cream of tartar
1 tsp. baking soda
1/4 tsp. salt
1/2 cup vegetable shortening
1/2 cup margarine, softened
1 1/2 cups white sugar
2 eggs
1 tsp. vanilla extract
2 (8 oz.) packages cream cheese, softened
1 cup white sugar
2 tsps. vanilla extract
3 large bananas, sliced, or as needed
1 tbsp. lemon juice, or as needed
1 (16 oz.) package fresh strawberries, sliced
1 (6 oz.) container fresh blueberries

Directions:

1. Preheat oven to 350 degrees F (175 degrees C).
2. Whisk the flour, cream of tartar, baking soda, and salt in a bowl.
3. In a large mixing bowl, mash the vegetable shortening and margarine together until thoroughly combined, and beat in 1 1/2 cup of sugar, eggs, and 1 tsp. of vanilla extract.
4. Mix in the flour mixture to make a workable dough, and spread the dough out in a rectangle shape onto an ungreased 12x17 inch baking sheet.
5. Bake in the preheated oven until very lightly browned, 8 to 10 minutes. Allow to cool completely.
6. While the cookie base is cooling, mash the cream cheese with 1 cup of sugar and 2 tsps. of vanilla extract in a bowl until smooth.
7. Place sliced bananas in a bowl, and gently toss with lemon juice to prevent browning.
8. To decorate the pizza, spread the cream cheese filling all over the cookie base in an even, smooth layer.
9. Place the blueberries in a square in neat, closely-spaced rows, in the left upper corner for blue stars.
10. Arrange alternating stripes of white bananas and red strawberry slices across the pizza. Refrigerate leftovers.

Red, White, and Blue Double Berry Coconut Pops

Ingredients:

1 1/2 cups hulled fresh strawberries, coarsely chopped
3 packets powdered stevia, divided
1 cup canned light coconut milk
1 tsp. pure vanilla extract
1 1/2 cups blueberries

Directions:

1. Puree the strawberries in a blender or food processor with 1 packet stevia (you will get about 1 cup of strawberry liquid).
2. Pour about 2 tbsps. into each of 9 popsicle molds (it should fill each mold about ⅓ of the way; if you have extra, pour it into the 10th mold). Freeze this layer until solid, or nearly solid for a more "tie-dyed" look.
3. Mix the coconut milk, 1 packet stevia, and vanilla.
4. Pour about 2 tbsps. into each of 9 popsicle molds (it should fill each mold about 1/3 of the way; if you have extra, pour it into the 10th mold).
5. Freeze this layer until slushy (about 10 minutes), then insert the wooden sticks and freeze until solid, or nearly solid for a more "tie-dyed" look.
6. Puree the blueberries in a blender or food processor with 1 packet stevia (you will get about 1 scant cup of blueberry liquid).
7. Pour about 2 tbsps. into each of 9 popsicle molds (it should fill each mold about 1/3 of the way; if you have extra, pour it into the 10th mold).
8. Make sure not to fill the molds over the "fill" line, since liquid expands as it freezes.
9. Freeze the pops until solid before unmolding. To easily unmold the popsicles, dip the bottoms in warm water and they should slide right out.

Red, White, and Blueberry Cheesecake Pie

Ingredients:

8 sheets phyllo dough
1/4 cup butter, melted
2 (8 oz.) packages cream cheese
1/2 cup white sugar
1 tsp. vanilla extract 2 eggs
2 cups fresh blueberries
1/2 cup strawberry jelly
1 cup heavy cream, whipped (optional)

Directions:

1. On a flat surface, place one sheet of phyllo dough.
2. Brush it with melted butter, and cover with another piece of phyllo.
3. Repeat until all 8 sheets are used.
4. Using kitchen scissors, cut layered phyllo into a 12- to 13-inch circle.
5. Carefully press circle into a greased 9-inch pie plate; gently fan edges. Bake in preheated oven until edges are just golden, 6 to 8 minutes; cool slightly on a wire rack.
6. Reduce oven temperature to 350 degrees F (175 degrees C).
7. In a medium bowl, beat cream cheese, sugar, and vanilla with an electric mixer until light and fluffy. Beat in eggs until well combined.
8. Fold in 1 cup of blueberries. Pour filling into prepared crust.
9. Bake at 350 degrees F (175 degrees C) until set, 40 to 50 minutes.
10. To prevent the crust from over-browning, gently cover pie with foil for the last 25 minutes of baking.
11. Cool completely on a wire rack.
12. In a small bowl, beat jelly until smooth; spread over cheese filling. Arrange 1 cup blueberries on top in a star pattern.

All American Apple Pie

Ingredients:

1 1/2 cups all-purpose flour
1/2 cup vegetable oil
2 tbsps. cold milk
1 1/2 tsps. white sugar
1 tsp. salt
6 Fuji apples, cored and sliced
3/4 cup white sugar
3 tbsps. all-purpose flour
3/4 tsp. ground cinnamon
1/2 tsp. ground nutmeg
1/2 cup all-purpose flour
1/2 cup white sugar
1/2 cup butter

Directions:

1. Preheat oven to 350 degrees F (175 degrees C).
2. To Make Crust: In a large bowl, mix together 1 1/2 cups flour, oil, milk, 1 1/2 tsps. sugar and salt until evenly blended. Pat mixture into a 9 inch pie pan, spreading the dough evenly over the bottom and up sides.
3. Crimp edges of the dough around the perimeter.
4. To Make Filling: Mix together 3/4 cup sugar, 3 tbsps. flour, cinnamon, and nutmeg. Sprinkle over apples and toss to coat. Spread evenly in unbaked pie shell.
5. To Make Topping: Using a pastry cutter, mix together 1/2 cup flour, 1/2 cup sugar and butter until evenly distributed and crumbly in texture.
6. Sprinkle over apples.
7. Put pie in the oven on a cookie sheet to catch the juices that may spill over. Bake 45 minutes.

Red, White and Blue Strawberry Shortcake

Ingredients:

1 (18.25 oz.) package yellow cake mix
1 (8 oz.) container frozen whipped topping, thawed
1 pint blueberries, rinsed and drained
2 pints fresh strawberries, rinsed and sliced

Directions:

1. Prepare cake according to package directions and bake in a 9x13 inch pan.
2. Cool completely.
3. Frost cake with whipped topping.
4. Place blueberries in a square in the corner, and arrange sliced strawberries as stripes to make an American flag.
5. Chill until serving.

Red, White, and Blue Potato Salad

Ingredients:

2 cups fingerling potatoes, halved lengthwise (about 10 oz.)
2 cups small red potatoes, quartered (about 10 oz.)
2 cups small blue potatoes, halved lengthwise (about 10 oz.)
1/4 cup finely chopped red onion
2 tbsps. chopped fresh parsley
1 tbsp. chopped fresh dill
1 tbsp. chopped fresh chives
3 hard-cooked large eggs, finely chopped
1/4 cup red wine vinegar
2 tbsps. olive oil
1 1/4 tsps. salt
2 tsps. Dijon mustard
1/2 tsp. freshly ground black pepper
1 garlic clove, minced

Directions:

1. Place fingerling and red potatoes in a saucepan; cover with water. Bring to a boil. Reduce heat; simmer 15 minutes or until tender.
2. Drain; cool slightly.
3. Place potatoes in a large bowl.
4. Place blue potatoes in a saucepan; cover with water.
5. Bring to a boil.
6. Reduce heat; simmer 10 minutes or until tender.
7. Drain; cool slightly.
8. Add blue potatoes, onion, parsley, dill, chives, and eggs to bowl; toss gently.
9. Combine vinegar and remaining ingredients.
10. Pour over potato mixture; toss gently to combine. Serve warm, at room temperature, or chilled.

Patriotic Fruit Salsa

Ingredients:

1 cup fresh blueberries
1 cup diced strawberries
1 cup diced jicama
1/3 cup chopped cilantro
1/4 cup finely chopped red onion
2 tbsps. finely chopped jalapeno pepper, stemmed and seeded
Juice of 1 large lime
Salt, to taste
Tortilla chips, for serving

Directions:

1. In a medium bowl, combine blueberries, strawberries, jicama, cilantro, red onion, jalapeno, and lime juice.
2. Stir until well combined.
3. Season with salt, to taste.
4. Serve with tortilla chips.

Patriotic Ice Cream Sandwiches

Cheesecake Ice Cream Ingredients:

8 oz. cream cheese
Zest of 1 lemon
1 cup sour cream
1/2 cup half-and-half
2/3 cup sugar
Pinch of salt

Red Velvet Shortbread Stars Ingredients:

1 cup unsalted butter, softened
2/3 cup sugar
1/4 tsp. kosher salt
2 c. all-purpose flour
4 tbsp. cocoa powder
2 tbsp. (1 oz.) red food coloring
1 tsp. pure vanilla extract
Red sugar, to sprinkle on top

Cheesecake Ice Cream Directions:

1. Cut cream cheese into small pieces and place into a blender or food processor. Add the lemon zest, sour cream, half-and-half, sugar, and salt. Puree until very smooth. No chunks!
2. Chill the mixture thoroughly in the refrigerator for 1 hour, then freeze it in your ice cream maker according to the manufacturer's instructions.
3. Line a 9" square pan with parchment paper and then spread the ice cream into the prepared pan, smoothing it out as much as possible. Freeze ice cream in the pan until it is completely frozen.
4. This will take at least 2 hours.

Red Velvet Shortbread Stars Directions:

1. In the bowl of a stand mixer, beat butter and sugar until the mixture is a bit fluffy. Add in the salt and flour and mix until just incorporated.
2. Then add the cocoa powder and mix again.
3. Carefully add the food coloring and vanilla, stirring until red coloring is evenly distributed.
4. Divide dough into 2 equal portions and pat each into a 4" round disc. Wrap each disc in plastic wrap and refrigerate for 2 hours.

5. Heat oven to 350 degrees F. Line a cookie sheet with parchment paper and set aside.
6. Lightly flour your work surface and rolling pin.
7. Remove one dough disc from the refrigerator and roll to about 1/4" thick.
8. If the dough is sticky, just pick it up and pat into a round, flour your surface again, and roll out the dough again. I found that this second rolling did the trick every time. With a small star shaped cookie cutter (mine measured 2-1/4" across), cut out star shapes and place them on your parchment lined cookie sheet.
9. Sprinkle with red sugar.
10. Bake for 11 to 13 minutes, taking care to not let the cookies brown. Let cookies rest on cookie sheet a couple minutes before removing to a wire rack to cool completely.
11. To assemble the patriotic ice cream sandwiches:
12. Cut the ice cream around the edge of the pan and then gently remove the frozen slab of ice cream using the parchment paper overhang
13. Dip the same star cookie cutter you used for the ice cream into a shallow bowl of hot water and start cutting out ice cream stars, dipping the cutter into the hot water in between each cut.
14. Turn a star cookie upside down and place an ice cream star on top of the cookie.
15. Top with another star cookie (right side up) and gently press together to make a sandwich. Repeat until all ice cream stars are used. You will have more star cookies than you need.
16. Immediately place the ice cream sandwiches in the freezer to freeze thoroughly. Keep frozen until ready to serve.

Red, White and Blue Ambrosia Salad

Ingredients:

1 pint heavy cream
1 tbsp. confectioners' sugar
2 cups sour cream
1 1/2 cups flaked coconut
1 (20 oz.) can crushed pineapple, drained
1 pint strawberries, hulled and sliced
1 pint fresh blueberries
3 cups miniature marshmallows

Directions:

1. Combine the heavy cream and confectioners' sugar in a large bowl.
2. Whip with an electric mixer until thick but not grainy.
3. Mix in sour cream.
4. Use a rubber spatula to fold in the flaked coconut, pineapple, strawberries, blueberries and marshmallows until everything is evenly distributed.
5. Cover and chill for at least 4 hours before serving. It tastes best if chilled overnight.

Red, White and Blue Slaw Salad

Ingredients:

12 slices bacon
6 cups shredded cabbage
1 cup coleslaw dressing
1/2 cup blue cheese, crumbled
1 cup cherry tomatoes, halved

Directions:

1. Place bacon in a large, deep skillet.
2. Cook over medium high heat until evenly brown.
3. Crumble and set aside.
4. In a large bowl, combine the bacon, cabbage and dressing.
5. Mix well.
6. Sprinkle with halved cherry tomatoes and blue cheese.
7. Refrigerate and serve chilled.

Classic American Potato Salad

Ingredients:

2 pounds red boiling potatoes, scrubbed
2 tbsps. red wine vinegar
1/2 tsp. salt
1/2 tsp. freshly ground black pepper
3 hard-cooked eggs
1 small celery stalk
1/4 cup chopped sweet pickle (not relish)
3 scallions
2 tbsps. chopped fresh parsley
1/2 cup mayonnaise
2 tbsps. Dijon-style mustard

Directions:

1. Place potatoes in a pot with water to cover.
2. Bring to a boil, cover and simmer, stirring to ensure even cooking, until a thin-bladed paring knife or a metal skewer inserted into a potato can be removed with no resistance, 25 to 30 minutes.
3. Drain, rinse under cold water and drain again. Cool slightly.
4. Cut warm potatoes into 3/4-inch dice with a serrated knife.
5. Layer them in a bowl, seasoning with vinegar, salt and pepper as you go.
6. Cut eggs, celery and pickle in 1/4-inch dice and thinly slice scallions.
7. Add to potatoes, along with parsley. Stir in mayonnaise and mustard until everything is combined. Chill, covered, before serving.

Flag Pizza

Ingredients:

3 small purple potatoes cooking spray
1 (13.8 oz.) can refrigerated pizza crust
1 1/2 tbsps. olive oil, divided, or as needed
25 slices pepperoni, or more as needed
1 cup Alfredo sauce
2 cups shredded Italian cheese blend
5 mini mozzarella balls, halved

Directions:

1. Place potatoes into a pot and cover with salted water; bring to a boil. Reduce heat to medium-low and simmer until tender, about 20 minutes. Drain and slice potatoes into 1/4-inch rounds.
2. Preheat oven to 400 degrees F (200 degrees C). Spray a large baking sheet with cooking spray.
3. Unroll the refrigerated pizza crust and spread it out in the baking sheet to fit to the edges. Brush the crust with about 1 tbsp. olive oil.
4. Bake in the preheated oven until lightly golden and slightly set, about 7 minutes.
5. Arrange pepperoni slices on a paper towel-lined, microwave-safe plate. Microwave pepperoni on high until heated through, about 30 seconds.
6. Spread Alfredo sauce over the baked crust; top with Italian cheese blend. Arrange potato rounds in the top left corner of the pizza, forming the blue portion of the flag.
7. Brush potatoes with remaining olive oil.
8. Place mozzarella ball halves on top of the potatoes to resemble the stars of the flag.
9. Arrange pepperoni slices, slightly overlapping, in rows across the pizza to resemble the stripes on the flag.
10. Bake pizza in the oven until the crust is golden brown and cheese is melted, about 10 minutes.

Fourth of July Toast

Ingredients:

Thick sliced bread
Raspberry or strawberry jam
Bananas
Blueberries

Directions:

1. Toast the bread.
2. Spread the jam on one side of the toast.
3. Lay the blueberries on the toast in a three by three row in the upper left hand corner of the toast.
4. Peel the banana then slice it in circles.
5. Cut the banana circles in half to make half-circles.
6. Lay three half circles of banana along the bottom of the toast in a row.
7. Cut one half circle in half again in to quarter circles.
8. Lay a quarter circle of banana to align with the bottom of the blueberries.
9. Lay a half circle of banana next to the quarter circle of banana.
10. Lay another quarter circle of banana next to the top of the toast next to the blueberries.
11. Lay a half circle of banana next to the quarter circle of banana you just layed down.
12. Serve and enjoy!

4th of July Trifle

Ingredients:

2 (8 oz.) packages cream cheese
2 cups confectioners' sugar
8 oz. sour cream
1/4 tsp. almond flavoring
1 tsp. vanilla
1/2 pint whipping cream
1 angel food cake (store bought is fine)
1 quart strawberry
1 quart blueberries
3/4 cup sugar
3 tbsps. almond flavoring

Directions:

1. Cream together cream cheese and confectioners sugar.
2. Add sour cream, vanilla and 1/4 tsp almond flavoring.
3. Set this mixture aside.
4. In separate bowl whip the whipping cream and add to cream cheese mixture.
5. Tear up angel food cake and mix in with cheese mixture.
6. In separate bowl (s) place strawberries and blueberries 3/4 cup sugar and 3 Tbsp almond flavoring.
7. (You can mix the berries together or keep separate, for a pretty red, white and blue look,if separate divide sugar and almond flavoring between the two bowls).
8. In a clear glass bowl alternate layers of the cream cheese mixtures and the berries.
9. Garnish the top with berries.
10. Refrigerate for a couple of hours.
11. This looks absolutely beautiful and taste just as great!
12. Peaches work really well with this as well.

Red, White and Blue Burgers

Ingredients:

1 lb. lean ground sirloin
salt
fresh ground black pepper
1 red bell pepper, stemmed, seeded and quartered
1 tsp. olive oil
4 hamburger buns
1 large sweet white onion (Vidalia or Walla Walla)
2 tbsps. crumbled blue cheese

Directions:

1. Preheat grill to medium-high heat.
2. Using your hands, lightly shape the ground sirloin into four 1/2-inch thick patties. Try to leave some air in the burger and avoid packing them too densely.
3. Season with salt and pepper.
4. Lightly drizzle the red pepper quarters with olive oil.
5. Cook the burgers on both sides over the hot grill for about 5 to 6 minutes per side for medium burgers.
6. At the same time, grill the peppers for 2 to 3 minutes on each side.
7. Lightly toast the buns on the grill.
8. Serve the burgers on toasted buns with grilled red peppers, slices of sweet white onion and crumbled blue cheese.

Patriotic Breakfast Buns

Dough Ingredients:

1 1/3 cups all-purpose flour
1 (1/4 oz.) envelope dry yeast
2 egg yolks
2 tbsps. sugar
2 tsps. salt
1 3/4 cups warm milk
4 tbsps. butter, melted

Filling Ingredients:

1/2 cup blueberries
1 1/2 cups strawberries
2 tbsps. butter, melted
4 tbsps. sugar
Store-bought icing, for decoration

Directions:

1. In one bowl, stir in flour, sugar, and dry yeast. In another bowl, stir in yolk and salt.
2. Add warmed milk to flour mixture stir them until it becomes shaggy dough.
3. Then knead them until smooth.
4. Add melted butter little by little.
5. Place dough out onto a floured work surface and knead until smooth and elastic, 10 to 15.
6. minute.
7. Place dough in a bowl, cover bowl with damp towel, let stand in warm spot until dough.
8. has double in size (approx. 1 1/2 hours).
9. Divide dough into 4 pieces. Roll two of them into 10"x 8". One of them into 12"x8".
10. Brush them with melted butter and sprinkled sugar.
11. Lay out sliced strawberries and roll them then cut in 2" each.
12. Roll remaining dough into 8"x8".
13. Brush with melted butter and sprinkled sugar.
14. Layout blueberries and roll it then cut 2" each.
15. Arrange buns like a American flag in a 9"x13" bake pan.
16. Cover loosely with damp towel.

17. Let stand in warm spot until roll have double in size, about 1 hour.
18. Preheat oven to 350 degrees F.
19. Bake until golden light brown, about 25 minutes.
20. Let it cool then pipe with store bought icing.

Patriotic Pancakes

Ingredients:

2cups baking mix (such as Bisquick)
1cup milk
2eggs

Directions:

1. Heat griddle or skillet over medium-high heat or electric griddle to 375 degrees F; grease with cooking spray, vegetable oil or shortening. (Surface is ready when a few drops of water sprinkled on it dance and disappear.)
2. 2Stir all ingredients until blended.
3. Pour by slightly less than 1/4 cupfuls onto hot griddle.
4. 3Cook until edges are dry. Turn; cook until golden.
Note: If you like thin pancakes, use 1 1/2 cups milk.

Firecracker Red White and Blue Cake

Ingredients:

1 box white cake mix
Water, vegetable oil and egg whites called for on cake mix box
Red food color
Blue food color
1 container (12 oz.) Whipped fluffy white frosting

Directions:

1. Heat oven to 325°F. Generously grease 12-cup fluted tube cake pan. Make cake batter as directed on box, using water, oil and egg whites. Pour 1 cup of the batter into small bowl; stir in red food color until well mixed.
2. Pour another cup of the batter into separate bowl; stir in blue food color until well mixed.
3. Pour red cake batter into bottom of pan.
4. Carefully pour remaining white batter over red batter in pan.
5. Carefully pour blue batter over white batter. (Blue batter does not need to cover white batter completely; it looks better if it just forms a ring in the center of the white batter.)
6. Bake as directed on box or until toothpick inserted near center comes out clean. Cool cake 5 minutes.
7. Meanwhile, place cooling rack over cookie sheet. Turn pan upside down onto cooling rack.
8. Cool cake completely, about 30 minutes.
9. When cake is cool, divide frosting evenly into 3 microwavable bowls.
10. Microwave 1 bowl of frosting uncovered on High a few seconds until smooth enough to drizzle over cake. With spoon, drizzle all of white frosting back and forth around cake in a striping pattern. Repeat microwaving second bowl of frosting until smooth.
11. Stir in a few drops blue food color until well blended.
12. Drizzle over cake, scattering frosting back and forth. Repeat with remaining bowl of frosting and red food color, making sure red, white and blue frostings can be seen on cake.
13. Let cake stand at room temperature until frosting is set before serving.

Red, White and Blue Cake Pops

Ingredients:

1 box cake mix (any flavor)
Water, vegetable oil and eggs called for on cake mix box
1 container (12 oz) Whipped frosting (any flavor)
1 bag (14 oz.) candy melts (any flavor)
1 tsp. shortening
Craft sticks (flat wooden sticks with round ends)
Assorted candy sprinkles
Block of white plastic foam

Directions:

1. Line several cookie sheets with waxed paper. Make and bake cake mix as directed on box for 13x9-inch pan, using water, oil and eggs. Cool completely, about 1 hour.
2. With fingers, crumble cake into large bowl. Add frosting; mix well with fingers until dough forms. Shape into quarter-size balls; place on cookie sheets. Freeze about 15 minutes.
3. When ready to assemble, in small microwavable bowl, microwave candy melts uncovered as directed on bag. Stir in shortening until smooth and mixture runs off spoon.
4. Remove cake pop balls from freezer. Dip tip of each craft stick into melted candy, then halfway into 1 cake ball; place on waxed paper-lined cookie sheet.
5. When all cake balls have sticks, gently swirl 1 cake ball in melted candy to coat well; allow candy to drip back into bowl. Dip ball into candy sprinkles to decorate; place in plastic foam to allow candy to harden.
6. Repeat with remaining cake balls and melted candy.

Red, White and Blueberry Chex Bars

Ingredients:

1/4 cup unsalted butter
1 bag (10 oz) miniature marshmallows
6 cups Corn Chex cereal
1 cup mixed freeze-dried berries (strawberries, raspberries, blueberries), plus additional for topping
1/3 cup plus 2 tbsps. white vanilla baking chips
1 tbsp. coconut oil

Directions:

1. Spray 8-inch square pan with cooking spray; line with cooking parchment paper, leaving an overhang of paper on two sides.
2. In 4-quart saucepan, heat butter and marshmallows over medium heat, stirring frequently, until melted and smooth.
3. Remove from heat; add cereal and freeze-dried berries, and stir to combine.
4. Fold in 1/3 cup of the chips.
5. They may melt a little, but that's okay.
6. Press mixture evenly into pan.
7. Sprinkle with additional berries.
8. In small microwavable bowl, mix 2 tbsps. chips with the coconut oil; microwave uncovered on high in 30-second bursts until melted and smooth when stirred. Drizzle over top of bars.
9. Let stand until firm before cutting, about 50 minutes.
10. Cut into 4 rows by 3 rows.

Red, White and Blue Pinwheel Icebox Cookies

Ingredients:

3 cups
all-purpose flour
1/2 tsp.
Baking powder
1/2 tsp.
Salt
1 cup
(2 sticks) unsalted butter
1 1/3 cups
sugar
2 large eggs
2 tsps.
vanilla extract
Red food coloring
Blue food coloring

Directions:

1. In a medium bowl, sift together the flour, baking powder and salt.
2. In the bowl of a stand mixer fitted with the paddle attachment, beat the butter until smooth, about 2 minutes. Add the sugar and continue beating until the mixture is light and fluffy, about 3 minutes. Add the eggs one at a time, beating between each addition, then add the vanilla.
3. Turn the mixer off.
4. Add the flour and then beat just until combined. Remove the dough and separate it into three equal pieces. Shape one piece of the dough into a 4- by 4-inch square, wrap it securely in plastic wrap and place it in the fridge. (This will be the white portion of the cookies.)
5. Return one of the remaining pieces of dough to the stand mixer bowl, and with the mixer on "low," add in the red food coloring until it reaches your desired color.
6. Remove the red dough, shape it into a 4- by 4-inch square, wrap it securely in plastic wrap and place it in the fridge. (This will be the red portion of the cookies). Clean out the bowl to remove any red food coloring residue.
7. Add the final piece of dough to the stand mixer bowl, and with the mixer on "low," add in the blue food coloring until it reaches your desired color.

8. Remove the blue dough, shape it into a 4- by 4-inch square, wrap it securely in plastic wrap and place it in the fridge. (This will be the blue portion of the cookies.)
9. Refrigerate the dough for 30 minutes.
10. Remove the dough from the fridge and cut each square in half to form two rectangles. Wrap half of each color of dough in plastic wrap and return it to the fridge. Place the red dough in between two pieces of wax paper and roll it into a rectangle about 1/8-inch thick. Roll out the white dough between two separate pieces of wax paper until it is a rectangle about 1/8-inch thick. Roll out the blue dough between two separate pieces of wax paper until it is a rectangle about 1/8-inch thick.
11. Peel the top layer of wax paper off of the red dough and then peel the wax paper off one side of the white dough and use the other side to transfer the white dough on top of the red dough.
12. Peel off the wax paper from one side of the blue dough and use the other side to transfer it atop the white dough.
13. Very lightly roll the three layers together.
14. Starting at the shorter end of the rectangle, roll the dough as tightly as possible into a log. Repeat the rolling and stacking process with the remaining dough in the fridge.
15. Wrap the logs in wax paper and then plastic wrap and refrigerate them for 1 hour.
16. Remove the dough logs and roll them on the counter several times so they don't develop a flat side. Alternately, stand the rolls up in glasses in the fridge. Refrigerate the dough for 4 more hours.
17. When ready to bake, preheat the oven to 350 degrees F and line two baking sheets with parchment paper. Remove the dough from the fridge and slice each log into 1/4-inch rounds.
18. Place the rounds about 2 inches apart on the baking sheets, as the cookies will expand when baked.
19. Bake the cookies for 9 to 11 minutes until pale golden, and then transfer them to a wrack to cool completely.

Red, White & Blue Pie

Ingredients:

1 box refrigerated pie crusts, softened as directed on box
3 lb. fresh strawberries
1/2 cup fresh blueberries
1 cup sugar
2 tbsps. cornstarch
1 1/2 cups water
1 box (4-serving size) strawberry-flavored gelatin

Directions:

1. Heat oven to 450 degrees F.
2. Place 1 crust in ungreased 9-inch glass pie plate. Press crust firmly against side and bottom. Fold excess crust under and press together to form thick crust edge; flute. Prick bottom and side with fork.
3. Unroll second crust onto wax paper. Using 2-inch star-shaped cookie cutter, cut stars from pie crust; place on cookie sheet. Bake stars about 5 minutes, crust 10 to 12 minutes or until light brown. Cool.
4. Meanwhile, clean and hull strawberries. Set strawberries, points up, on paper towel to dry. Wash blueberries, dry on paper towel.
5. Place strawberries point sides up in baked pie shell; place blueberries between strawberries. Set aside.
6. In 2 quart saucepan, stir together sugar and cornstarch. Stir in water; heat to rolling boil. Cook a full 2 minutes.
7. Remove from heat; stir in gelatin.
8. Cool 15 to 20 minutes. Spoon over berries in crust, making sure each piece is covered. Chill at least 4 hours or overnight.
9. Top each serving with star cutouts.

Patriotic Oatmeal Cookies

Ingredients:

1 cup butter, room temperature
1 cup sugar
1 cup brown sugar
2 large eggs
2 tsp vanilla extract
2 cups all-purpose flour
1 tsp baking soda
1 tsp baking powder
1 tsp salt
2 1/2 cups oatmeal (rolled or quick cooking, not instant)
2/3 cup each raisins, dried cranberries and dried blueberries

Directions:

1. Preheat the oven to 350F. Line a baking sheet with parchment paper.
2. In a large bowl, cream together the butter and the sugars until mixture is light. Beat in the eggs one at a time, followed by the vanilla extract.
3. In a medium bowl, whisk together the flour, baking soda, baking powder and salt. Gradually blend the flour mixture into butter mixture.
4. Stir in the oats and dried fruits.
5. Drop 1-inch balls of dough onto the cookie sheet, placing about 1 1/2 inches apart so they have room to spread.
6. Bake at 350F for 10-13 minutes, until cookies are just golden brown at the edges.
7. Cool on baking sheet for at least 1-2 minutes before transferring to a wire rack to cool completely.

Patriotic M&M Cookies

Ingredients:

1 cup brown sugar, lightly packed
1/2 cup granulated sugar
1 tsp. salt
2 eggs, large
1 tsp. vanilla extract
3 cups flour, unbleached or all-purpose
1 tsp. baking powder
1 tsp. baking soda
1 1/2 cups mini red, white and blue coated milk chocolate candies, such as M&M'S, reserve 1/4 cup

Directions:

1. Preheat an oven to 360 degrees F.
2. In a large mixing bowl, cream the butter, sugars and salt.
3. Mix on low speed for about a minute, then on medium speed for another minute.
4. Add the eggs & vanilla extract. Mix on low until the eggs are blended in, then at medium speed for a minute and then on high speed for an additional minute. The mixture should be a pale yellow color and very fluffy.
5. Add the first cup of flour, along with the baking powder and baking soda. Then add the remainder of the flour a cup at a time.
6. Mix in the chocolate candies on low speed, reserving 1/4 cup for the tops.
7. Using a 2 oz. cookie scooper, place dough on ungreased baking sheets about 2" a part.
8. Place a few M&M'S mini milk chocolate candies on the tops where needed.
9. Bake in a preheated 360 degrees F oven for 10-12 minutes, or until the tops start to crackle and the cookies are light golden brown.
10. Cool on baking sheets for 10 minutes before transferring them to a cooling rack.

Patriotic Brownie Pizza

Ingredients:

1 box (1 lb. 6.25 oz.) brownie mix
Water, vegetable oil and eggs called for on brownie mix box
1 package (8 oz.) cream cheese, softened
1/3 cup sugar
1/2 tsp. vanilla
2 cups sliced fresh strawberries
1 cup fresh blueberries
1 cup fresh raspberries
1/2 cup apple jelly

Directions:

1. Heat oven to 350°F (325°F for dark or nonstick pan).
2. Grease bottom only of 12x3/4-inch pizza pan with shortening or cooking spray.
3. Make brownie batter as directed on box. Spread in pan.
4. Bake 25 to 28 minutes or until toothpick inserted 2 inches from side of pan comes out almost clean.
5. Cool completely, about 1 hour.
6. In small bowl, beat cream cheese, sugar and vanilla with electric mixer on medium speed until smooth.
7. Carefully spread mixture evenly over brownie base. Arrange berries over cream cheese mixture
8. Stir jelly until smooth; brush over berries. Refrigerate about 1 hour or until chilled.
9. Cut into wedges.

Patriotic Berry Bars

Ingredients:

1 box yellow cake mix
1 cup butter or margarine, softened
2 eggs
1 container whipped fluffy white frosting
4 cups fresh berries (sliced strawberries, raspberries and blueberries)

Directions:

1. Heat oven to 350 degrees F (325 degrees F for dark or nonstick pan).
2. Spray 15x10x1-inch pan with baking spray with flour.
3. In large bowl, beat cake mix, softened butter and eggs with electric mixer on medium speed about 1 minute or until well blended. Spread evenly in pan.
4. Bake 19 to 24 minutes or until top is evenly golden brown and toothpick inserted in center comes out clean. Cool completely, about 1 hour.
5. Spread frosting evenly over cooled bars.
6. Top with berries up to 2 hours before serving. For 48 bars, cut into 8 rows by 6 rows.

Patriotic Berry Cream Torte

Ingredients:

1 box white cake mix
Water, vegetable oil and egg whites called for on cake mix box
2 containers whipped fluffy white frosting
1 container (8 oz.) frozen whipped topping, thawed
1 cup fresh raspberries
1 cup fresh blueberries
1 cup sliced fresh strawberries
1/4 cup seedless strawberry jam
1 tbsp. orange juice

Directions:

1. Heat oven to 350 degrees F (325 degrees F for dark or nonstick pans). Make, bake and cool cake as directed on box for two 8-inch or 9-inch round cake pans.
2. In large bowl, mix frosting and whipped topping until well blended.
3. To assemble cake, cut each layer in half horizontally.
4. Place 1 layer half on serving plate; spread with 1 cup of the frosting mixture.
5. Repeat 3 more times.
6. Arrange berries on top of cake.
7. In small microwavable bowl, microwave jam uncovered on High about 20 seconds or until warm.
8. Stir in orange juice; mix well with fork. Brush over berries.

Patriotic Cupcake Sandwiches

Cupcake Ingredients:

1 box white cake mix
Any ingredients called for on the cake mix box (water, vegetable oil, egg whites)
Food colors in red and blue.

Frosting Ingredients:

1 1/2 cups marshmallow creme
3/4 cup butter, softened
1 1/4 cups powdered sugar
Food colors in red and blue.

Directions:

1. Heat oven to 350 degrees F (for all pans).
2. Spray 60 mini muffin cups. Make cake batter as directed on box.
3. Divide batter among 3 small bowls.
4. Make 3 different colors of batter by adding 1/4 tsp. food color to each bowl for the red and blue, but leave the third bowl white.
5. Blend well.
6. Fill each muffin cup with 1 level measuring tbsp. batter, making an even number of cupcakes of each color.
7. Bake 11 to 14 minutes or until toothpick inserted in center comes out clean.
8. Cool 5 minutes; remove from pan.
9. Cool completely, about 10 minutes.
10. In large bowl, beat marshmallow creme and butter with electric mixer on medium speed until blended.
11. Beat in powdered sugar until fluffy.
12. Divide frosting among 3 small bowls.
13. Using the same food colors as before, lightly tint frosting in each bowl to match the red and blue cupcake colors, but leave the third one white.
14. Assemble each sandwich using 2 mini cupcakes.
15. Cut tops off each cupcake horizontally (discard bottoms).
16. Spread or pipe about 1 tbsp. frosting on cut side of 1 cupcake top.
17. Form a sandwich by placing cut side of second cupcake top on frosting.
18. Press lightly.
19. Repeat with remaining cupcake tops.

Patriotic Watermelon Sangria

Ingredients:

1 Large watermelon
1 750-ml bottle white wine
2 c. white rum
1 c. Seltzer
1/3 c. lime juice (from about 6 limes)
2 limes, thinly sliced
2 c. assorted fresh or frozen fruit, such as pineapple, blueberries, and strawberries

Directions:

1. Slice off the top third of the watermelon lengthwise (save for later use) and score fruit with a knife. Using a large spoon or ice cream scoop, scoop out watermelon and transfer to blender.
2. Blend watermelon until smooth. (If desired, strain seeds.)
3. Add white wine, rum, seltzer, and lime juice and stir until combined, then add limes and fruit.
4. Refrigerate until chilled, about 2 hours, then serve.

Patriotic Caprese Tomatoes

Ingredients:

6 oz. fresh mozzarella, sliced into small rounds
2 tbsp. extra-virgin olive oil
1 tsp. Italian seasoning
1 tsp. flaky sea salt
Freshly ground black pepper
6 plum tomatoes
6 Fresh basil leaves, torn
Balsamic glaze, for serving

Directions:

1. Combine mozzarella, olive oil, Italian seasoning and salt in a small bowl. Season to taste with pepper and let marinate while you prepare the tomatoes.
2. Slice each tomato crosswise, like an accordion, making sure not to cut all the way through tomato.
3. Place cut tomatoes on a serving platter.
4. Insert marinated cheese slices and pieces of torn basil into each slit.
5. Drizzle the tomatoes with balsamic glaze and serve immediately.

Patriotic Bark

Ingredients:

1 cup white candy melts, melted
1 cup blue candy melts, melted
1 cup red candy melts, melted
1/3 cup red, white and blue sprinkles
2 tbsp. edible gold stars (available at craft stores)
2 tbsp. blue edible glitter (available at craft stores)

Directions:

1. On a baking sheet, add spoonfuls of melted white, blue and red candy melts, adding twice as many white spoonfuls than red and blue.
2. Using an offset spatula or knife, swirl colors together, creating a tie-dye effect.
3. Top with sprinkles and edible gold stars and glitter.
4. Freeze 20 minutes.
5. Break into pieces and serve.

Patriotic Sweet and Salty Cereal Bars

Ingredients:

4 cups Honey Nut Cheerios cereal
1 cup dry-roasted peanuts
1 cup candy coated chocolate candies (such as M&Ms) red, white and blue only
1 cup pretzel sticks, coarsely broken
1/3 cup packed brown sugar
1/3 cup light corn syrup
1 tbsp. butter

Directions:

1. Line bottom and sides of 8-inch square pan with foil or parchment paper. Spray foil with cooking spray. In large bowl, mix cereal, peanuts, chocolate candies and pretzels; set aside.
2. In large microwavable bowl, microwave brown sugar, corn syrup and butter uncovered on High 2 to 3 minutes, stirring every 30 seconds, until mixture is boiling.
3. Microwave an additional 1 minute allowing mixture to boil and thicken slightly. Let stand 3 minutes to cool slightly.
1. Pour over cereal mixture in bowl; stir until evenly coated. Using buttered back of spoon, press mixture very firmly in pan. Refrigerate about 1 hour or until firm enough to cut.
2. For bars, cut into 4 rows by 4 rows. Store covered at room temperature up to 1 week.

Freedom Cookie Pops

Ingredients:

11 oz. white chocolate
1/3 cup pretzels
1/3 cup roasted almonds, roughly chopped
1/4 cup mini M&M's
2 tbsp. red, white, and blue confetti

Directions:

1. Line baking sheet with parchment paper. Insert popsicle stick into center of cookie; set aside.
2. Place white chocolate in heat-proof bowl over pan of simmering water. Stir continuously until melted.
3. For ease of dipping, transfer chocolate to deep heat-proof vessel.
4. Dip cookies in white chocolate and place on parchment-lined baking sheet. Sprinkle with both sanding sugars and star sprinkles.
5. Transfer to refrigerator for chocolate to set, about 20 minutes.
6. Keep chilled until ready to serve.
7. If you want to take the cute factor up a notch, wrap washi tape around popsicle stick for a decorative finish.

Celebration Boozy Cherry Bombs

Ingredients:

1 jar maraschino cherries with stems
1 cup Fireball whisky
1 cup whipped cream-flavored vodka
1 cup white chocolate chips
1 jar blue sanding sugar sprinkles

Directions:

1. Soak cherries in equal parts Fireball and vodka for 1 hour in the refrigerator.
2. Remove cherries and pat dry with a paper towel.
3. Heat chocolate chips in the microwave in 20-second intervals, stirring in between, until fully melted.
4. Dip each cherry two-thirds of the way into the melted white chocolate, twisting it slightly to help the chocolate stick.
5. Dip the cherry in blue sanding sugar, coating it halfway up the white chocolate coating.
6. Chill in fridge 20 minutes before serving.

Party Grilled Brie

Ingredients:

1 Wheel of Brie
1/4 cup olive oil, divided
1 cup chopped strawberries
1 French baguette, sliced
2 tbsp. thinly sliced basil
2 tbsp. balsamic glaze

Directions:

1. Heat grill to medium-low.
2. Place cheese on a large piece of foil. Drizzle with about a tbsp. of olive oil. Top the cheese with strawberries, then fold foil to cover the cheese completely.
3. Brush baguette slices with remaining olive oil.
4. Place the foil-wrapped brie and bread on the grill. Grill the cheese until melted, about 5-10 minutes, depending on the size of the wheel.
5. Check it every few minutes.
6. When it feels loose and soft to touch, it's time to remove from the grill.
7. Flip the baguette slices as they turn golden brown, about 2 minutes and transfer toasted pieces to a platter.
8. Drizzle the melted, grilled brie with balsamic glaze and sprinkle basil on top. Enjoy with grilled bread.

Firecracker Milkshake

Ingredients:

1 half gal. vanilla ice cream
2-3 drops red food coloring
2-3 drops blue food coloring

Directions:

1. Soften ice cream to a soft serve/yogurt texture. Evenly divide ice cream into three bowls.
2. Place red food coloring in one bowl and blue food coloring in the other, using a whisk beat each bowl until color is well blended.
3. Layer bottom of glass with red ice cream, then plain vanilla and blue ice cream, using long spoon or knife drag it from the bottom to the top, stirring in between to mix the color (do not overmix).
4. Optional decorating idea: Finish with whipped cream and red, white and blue confetti

About the Author

Laura Sommers is **The Recipe Lady!**

She is the #1 Best Selling Author of over 80 recipe books.

She is a loving wife and mother who lives on a small farm in Baltimore County, Maryland and has a passion for all things domestic especially when it comes to saving money. She has a profitable eBay business and is a couponing addict. Follow her tips and tricks to learn how to make delicious meals on a budget, save money or to learn the latest life hack!

Visit her Amazon Author Page to see her latest books:

amazon.com/author/laurasommers

Visit the Recipe Lady's blog for even more great recipes and to learn which books are **FREE** for download each week:

http://the-recipe-lady.blogspot.com/

Subscribe to The Recipe Lady blog through Amazon and have recipes and updates sent directly to your Kindle:

The Recipe Lady Blog through Amazon

Laura Sommers is also an Extreme Couponer and Penny Hauler! If you would like to find out how to get things for **FREE** with coupons or how to get things for only a **PENNY**, then visit her couponing blog **Penny Items and Freebies**

http://penny-items-and-freebies.blogspot.com/

Other Cookbooks by Laura Sommers

- **Recipes for Chicken Wings**
- **Party Dip Recipes for the Big Game**
- **50 Super Awesome Salsa Recipes!**
- **Easy to Make Party Dip Recipes: Chips and Dips and Salsa and Whips!**
- **Super Summer Barbecue and Pool Party Picnic Salad Recipes!**
- **50 Super Awesome Coleslaw and Potato Salad Recipes**
- **Homemade Salad Dressing Recipes from Scratch!**
- **50 Super Awesome Pasta Salad Recipes!**
- **50 Delicious Homemade Ice Cream Recipes**

May all of your meals be a banquet
with good friends and good food.

Made in the USA
Lexington, KY
19 June 2017